VERSES.

By SUSAN COOLIDGE.

BOSTON:
ROBERTS BROTHERS.
1880.

Copyright, 1880,
By Roberts Brothers.

University Press:
John Wilson and Son, Cambridge.

TO J. H. AND E. W. H.

Nourished by peaceful suns and gracious dew,
Your sweet youth budded and your sweet lives grew,
And all the world seemed rose-beset for you.

The rose of beauty was your mutual dower,
The stainless rose of love, an early flower,
The stately blooms of ease and wealth and power.

And treading thus on pathways flower-bestrewn,
It well might be, that, cold and careless grown,
You both had lived for your own joys alone.

But, holding all these fair things as in trust,
Gently you walked, still scattering on the dust
Of harder roads, which others tread, and must, —

Your heritage of brightness; not a ray
Of noontide sought you out, but straight away
You caught and halved it with some darker day:

And as the sweet saint's loaves were turned, 't is said,
To roses, so your roses turned to bread,
That hungering souls and weary might be fed.

Dear friends, my poor words do but paint you wrong,
Nor can I utter, in one trivial song,
The goodness I have honored for so long.

Only this leaf, a single petal flung,
One chord from a full harmony unsung,
May speak the life-long love that lacks a tongue.

CONTENTS.

PRELUDE.

OEMS are heavenly things,
And only souls with wings
May reach them where they grow,
May pluck and bear below,
Feeding the nations thus
With food all glorious.

Verses are not of these ;
They bloom on earthly trees,
Poised on a low-hung stem,
And those may gather them
Who cannot fly to where
The heavenly gardens are.

So I by devious ways
Have pulled some easy sprays

From the down-dropping bough
Which all may reach, and now
I knot them, bud and leaf,
Into a rhymèd sheaf.

Not mine the pinion strong
To win the nobler song;
I only cull and bring
A hedge-row offering
Of berry, flower, and brake,
If haply some may take.

VERSES.

COMMISSIONED.

"Do their errands; enter into the sacrifice with them; be a link yourself in the divine chain, and feel the joy and life of it." — ADELINE D. T. WHITNEY.

WHAT can I do for thee, Beloved,
  Whose feet so little while ago
  Trod the same way-side dust with mine,
And now up paths I do not know
  Speed, without sound or sign?

What can I do? The perfect life
  All fresh and fair and beautiful
  Has opened its wide arms to thee;
Thy cup is over-brimmed and full;
  Nothing remains for me.

I used to do so many things, —
  Love thee and chide thee and caress;
  Brush little straws from off thy way,
Tempering with my poor tenderness
  The heat of thy short day.

Not much, but very sweet to give;
  And it is grief of griefs to bear
  That all these ministries are o'er,
And thou, so happy, Love, elsewhere,
  Never can need me more: —

And I can do for thee but this
  (Working on blindly, knowing not
  If I may give thee pleasure so):
Out of my own dull, burdened lot
  I can arise, and go

To sadder lives and darker homes,
  A messenger, dear heart, from thee
  Who wast on earth a comforter;
And say to those who welcome me,
  I am sent forth by her.

Feeling the while how good it is
  To do thy errands thus, and think
  It may be, in the blue, far space,
Thou watchest from the heaven's brink, —
  A smile upon my face.

And when the day's work ends with day,
  And star-eyed evening, stealing in,
  Waves a cool hand to flying noon,
And restless, surging thoughts begin,
  Like sad bells out of tune,

I 'll pray: "Dear Lord, to whose great love
  Nor bound nor limit line is set,
  Give to my darling, I implore,
Some new sweet joy not tasted yet,
  For I can give no more."

And with the words my thoughts shall climb
  With following feet the heavenly stair
  Up which thy steps so lately sped,
And, seeing thee so happy there,
  Come back half comforted.

THE CRADLE TOMB IN WESTMINSTER ABBEY.

LITTLE, rudely sculptured bed,
  With shadowing folds of marble lace,
And quilt of marble, primly spread
  And folded round a baby's face.

Smoothly the mimic coverlet,
  With royal blazonries bedight,
Hangs, as by tender fingers set
  And straightened for the last good-night.

And traced upon the pillowing stone
  A dent is seen, as if to bless
The quiet sleep some grieving one
  Had leaned, and left a soft impress.

It seems no more than yesterday
  Since the sad mother down the stair
And down the long aisle stole away,
  And left her darling sleeping there.

But dust upon the cradle lies,
  And those who prized the baby so,
And laid her down to rest with sighs,
  Were turned to dust long years ago.

Above the peaceful pillowed head
  Three centuries brood, and strangers peep
And wonder at the carven bed, —
  But not unwept the baby's sleep,

For wistful mother-eyes are blurred
  With sudden mists, as lingerers stay,
And the old dusts are roused and stirred
  By the warm tear-drops of to-day.

Soft, furtive hands caress the stone,
  And hearts, o'erleaping place and age,
Melt into memories, and own
  A thrill of common parentage.

Men die, but sorrow never dies ;
  The crowding years divide in vain,
And the wide world is knit with ties
  Of common brotherhood in pain ;

Of common share in grief and loss,
  And heritage in the immortal bloom
Of Love, which, flowering round its cross,
  Made beautiful a baby's tomb.

"OF SUCH AS I HAVE."

LOVE me for what I am, Love. Not for sake
Of some imagined thing which I might be,
Some brightness or some goodness not in me,
Born of your hope, as dawn to eyes that wake
Imagined morns before the morning break.
If I, to please you (whom I fain would please),
Reset myself like new key to old tune,
Chained thought, remodelled action, very soon
My hand would slip from yours, and by degrees
The loving, faulty friend, so close to-day,
Would vanish, and another take her place, —
A stranger with a stranger's scrutinies,
A new regard, an unfamiliar face.
Love me for what I am, then, if you may;
But, if you cannot, — love me either way.

A PORTRAIT.

ALL sweet and various things do lend themselves
   And blend and intermix in her rare soul,
As chorded notes, which were untuneful else,
   Clasp each the other in a perfect whole.

Within her spirit, dawn, all dewy-pearled,
   Seems held and folded in by golden noons,
While past the sunshine gleams a further world
   Of deep star-spaces and mysterious moons.

Like widths of blowing ocean wet with spray,
   Like breath of early blooms at morning caught,
Like cool airs on the cheek of heated day,
   Come the fair emanations of her thought.

Her movement, like the curving of a vine,
   Seems an unerring accident of grace,
And like a flower 's the subtle change and shine
   And meaning of her brightly tranquil face.

And like a tree, unconscious of her shade,
She spreads her helpful branches everywhere
For wandering bird or bee, nor is afraid
Too many guests shall crowd to harbor there.

For she is kinder than all others are,
And weak things, sad things, gather where she dwells,
To reach and taste her strength and drink of her,
As thirsty creatures of clear water-wells.

Why vex with words where words are poor and vain?
In one brief sentence lies the riddle's key,
Which those who love her read and read again,
Finding each time new meanings: *She is she!*

WHEN?

F I were told that I must die to-morrow,
That the next sun
Which sinks should bear me past all fear and sorrow
For any one,
All the fight fought, all the short journey through:
What should I do?

I do not think that I should shrink or falter,
But just go on,
Doing my work, nor change, nor seek to alter
Aught that is gone;
But rise and move and love and smile and pray
For one more day.

And, lying down at night for a last sleeping,
Say in that ear
Which hearkens ever: "Lord, within Thy keeping
How should I fear?
And when to-morrow brings Thee nearer still,
Do Thou Thy will."

I might not sleep for awe; but peaceful, tender,
My soul would lie
All the night long; and when the morning splendor
Flushed o'er the sky,
I think that I could smile — could calmly say,
"It is His day."

But, if instead a hand from the blue yonder
Held out a scroll,
On which my life was writ, and I with wonder
Beheld unroll
To a long century's end its mystic clew,
What should I do?

What *could* I do, O blessed Guide and Master,
Other than this:
Still to go on as now, not slower, faster,
Nor fear to miss
The road, although so very long it be,
While led by Thee?

Step after step, feeling Thee close beside me,
Although unseen,

Through thorns, through flowers, whether the tempest
hide Thee,
Or heavens serene,
Assured Thy faithfulness cannot betray,
Thy love decay.

I may not know, my God; no hand revealeth
Thy counsels wise;
Along the path a deepening shadow stealeth,
No voice replies
To all my questioning thought, the time to tell,
And it is well.

Let me keep on, abiding and unfearing
Thy will always,
Through a long century's ripening fruition,
Or a short day's.
Thou canst not come too soon; and I can wait
If thou come late.

ON THE SHORE.

THE punctual tide draws up the bay,
With ripple of wave and hiss of spray,
And the great red flower of the light-house tower
Blooms on the headland far away.

Petal by petal its fiery rose
Out of the darkness buds and grows;
A dazzling shape on the dim, far cape,
A beckoning shape as it comes and goes.

A moment of bloom, and then it dies
On the windy cliff 'twixt the sea and skies.
The fog laughs low to see it go,
And the white waves watch it with cruel eyes.

Then suddenly out of the mist cloud dun,
As touched and wooed by unseen sun,
Again into sight bursts the rose of light
And opens its petals one by one.

Ah, the storm may be wild and the sea be strong,
And man is weak and the darkness long,
But while blossoms the flower on the light-house tower
There still is place for a smile and a song.

AMONG THE LILIES.

SHE stood among the lilies
In sunset's brightest ray,
Among the tall June lilies,
As stately fair as they;
And I, a boyish lover then,
Looked once, and, lingering, looked again,
And life began that day.

She sat among the lilies,
My sweet, all lily-pale;
The summer lilies listened,
I whispered low my tale.
O golden anthers, breathing balm,
O hush of peace, O twilight calm,
Did you or I prevail?

She lies among the lily-snows,
Beneath the wintry sky;

All round her and about her
The buried lilies lie.
They will awake at touch of Spring,
And she, my fair and flower-like thing,
In spring-time — by and by.

NOVEMBER.

DRY leaves upon the wall,
Which flap like rustling wings and seek escape,
A single frosted cluster on the grape
Still hangs — and that is all.

It hangs forgotten quite, —
Forgotten in the purple vintage-day,
Left for the sharp and cruel frosts to slay,
The daggers of the night.

It knew the thrill of spring;
It had its blossom-time, its perfumed noons;
Its pale-green spheres were rounded to soft runes
Of summer's whispering.

Through balmy morns of May;
Through fragrances of June and bright July,
And August, hot and still, it hung on high
And purpled day by day.

Of fair and mantling shapes,
No braver, fairer cluster on the tree;
And what then is this thing has come to thee
Among the other grapes,

Thou lonely tenant of the leafless vine,
Granted the right to grow thy mates beside,
To ripen thy sweet juices, but denied
Thy place among the wine?

Ah! we are dull and blind.
The riddle is too hard for us to guess
The why of joy or of unhappiness,
Chosen or left behind.

But everywhere a host
Of lonely lives shall read their type in thine:
Grapes which may never swell the tale of wine,
Left out to meet the frost.

EMBALMED.

THIS is the street and the dwelling,
  Let me count the houses o'er;
Yes, — one, two, three from the corner,
  And the house that I love makes four.

That is the very window
  Where I used to see her head
Bent over book or needle,
  With ivy garlanded.

And the very loop of the curtain,
  And the very curve of the vine,
Were full of the grace and the meaning
  Which was hers by some right divine.

I began to be glad at the corner,
  And all the way to the door
My heart outran my footsteps,
  And frolicked and danced before,

In haste for the words of welcome,
  The voice, the repose and grace,
And the smile, like a benediction,
  Of that beautiful, vanished face.

Now I pass the door, and I pause not,
  And I look the other way ;
But ever, a waft of fragrance,
  Too subtle to name or stay,

Comes the thought of the gracious presence
  Which made that past time sweet,
And still to those who remember,
  Embalms the house and the street,

Like the breath from some vase, now empty
  Of a flowery shape unseen,
Which follows the path of its lover,
  To tell where a rose has been.

GINEVRA DEGLI AMIERI.

A STORY OF OLD FLORENCE.

SO it is come! The doctor's glossy smile
Deceives me not. I saw him shake his head,
Whispering, and heard poor Giulia sob without,
As, slowly creaking, he went down the stair.
Were they afraid that I should be afraid?
I, who had died once and been laid in tomb?
They need not.

Little one, look not so pale.
I am not raving. Ah! you never heard
The story. Climb up there upon the bed:
Sit close, and listen. After this one day
I shall not tell you stories any more.

How old are you, my rose? What! almost twelve?
Almost a woman? Scarcely more than that

Was your fair mother when she bore her bud;
And scarcely more was I when, long years since,
I left my father's house, a bride in May.
You know the house, beside St. Andrea's church,
Gloomy and rich, which stands, and seems to frown
On the Mercato, humming at its base;
And hold on high, out of the common reach,
The lilies and carved shields above its door;
And, higher yet, to catch and woo the sun,
A little *loggia* set against the sky?
That was my play-place ever as a child;
And with me used to play a kinsman's son,
Antonio Rondinelli. Ah, dear days!
Two happy things we were, with none to chide
Or hint that life was anything but play.

Sudden the play-time ended. All at once
"You must be wed," they told me. "What is wed?"
I asked; but with the word I bent my brow,
Let them put on the garland, smiled to see
The glancing jewels tied about my neck;
And so, half-pleased, half-puzzled, was led forth
By my grave husband, older than my sire.

O the long years that followed! It would seem
That the sun never shone in all those years,
Or only with a sudden, troubled glint
Flashed on Antonio's curls, as he went by
Doffing his cap, with eyes of wistful love
Raised to my face, — my conscious, woful face.
Were we so much to blame? Our lives had twined
Together, none forbidding, for so long.
They let our childish fingers drop the seed,
Unhindered, which should ripen to tall grain;
They let the firm, small roots tangle and grow,
Then rent them, careless that it hurt the plant.
I loved Antonio, and he loved me.

Life was all shadow, but it was not sin!
I loved Antonio; but I kept me pure,
Not for my husband's sake, but for the sake
Of him, my first-born child, my little child,
Mine for a few short weeks, whose touch, whose look
Thrilled all my soul and thrills it to this day.
I loved; but, hear me swear, I kept me pure!
(Remember that, Madonna, when I come
Before thy throne to-morrow. Be not stern,
Or gaze upon me with reproachful look,

Making my little angel hide his face
And weep, while all the others turn glad eyes
Rejoicing on their mothers.)

It was hard
To sit in darkness while the rest had light,
To move to discords when the rest had song,
To be so young and never to have lived.
I bore, as women bear, until one day
Soul said to flesh, "This I endure no more,"
And with the word uprose, tore clay apart,
And what was blank before grew blanker still.

It was a fever, so the leeches said.
I had been dead so long, I did not know
The difference, or heed. Oil on my breast,
The garments of the grave about me wrapped,
They bore me forth, and laid me in the tomb,
The rich and beautiful and dreadful tomb,
Where all the buried Amieris lie,
Beneath the Duomo's black and towering shade.

Open the curtain, child. Yes, it is night.
It was night then, when I awoke to feel
That deadly chill, and see by ghostly gleams

Of moonlight, creeping through the grated door,
The coffins of my fathers all about.
Strange, hollow clamors rang and echoed back,
As, struggling out of mine, I dropped and fell.
With frantic strength I beat upon the grate.
It yielded to my touch. Some careless hand
Had left the bolt half-slipped. My father swore
Afterward, with a curse, he would make sure
Next time. *Next time.* That hurts me even now!

Dead or alive I issued, scarce sure which.
High overhead Giotto's tower soared;
Behind, the Duomo rose all white and black;
Then pealed a sudden jargoning of bells,
And down the darkling street I wildly fled,
Led by a little, cold, and wandering moon,
Which seemed as lonely and as lost as I.
I had no aim, save to reach warmth and light
And human touch; but still my witless steps
Led to my husband's door, and there I stopped,
By instinct, knocked, and called.

A window oped.
A voice — 'twas his — demanded: "Who is there?"
"'T is I, Ginevra." Then I heard the tone

Change into horror, and he prayed aloud
And called upon the saints, the while I urged,
" O, let me in, Francesco ; let me in !
I am so cold, so frightened, let me in ! "
Then, with a crash, the window was shut fast ;
And, though I cried and beat upon the door
And wailed aloud, no other answer came.

Weeping, I turned away, and feebly strove
Down the hard distance towards my father's house.
"They will have pity and will let me in,"
I thought. "They loved me and will let me in."
Cowards ! At the high window overhead
They stood and trembled, while I plead and prayed :
" I am your child, Ginevra. Let me in !
I am not dead. In mercy, let me in ! "
"The holy saints forbid ! " declared my sire.
My mother sobbed and vowed whole pounds of wax
To St. Eustachio, would he but remove
This fearful presence from her door. Then sharp
Came click of lock, and a long tube was thrust
From out the window, and my brother cried,
" Spirit or devil, go ! or else I fire ! "

Where should I go? Back to the ghastly tomb
And the cold coffined ones? Up the long street,
Wringing my hands and sobbing low, I went.
My feet were bare and bleeding from the stones;
My hands were bleeding too; my hair hung loose
Over my shroud. So wild and strange a shape
Saw never Florence since. The people call
That street through which I walked and wrung my hands
"Street of the Dead One," even to this day.
The sleeping houses stood in midnight black,
And not a soul was in the streets but I.

At last I saw a flickering point of light
High overhead, in a dim window set.
I had lain down to die; but at the sight
I rose, crawled on, and with expiring strength
Knocked, sank again, and knew not even then
It was Antonio's door by which I lay.

A window opened, and a voice called out:
"*Qui è?*" "I am Ginevra." And I thought,
"Now he will fall to trembling, like the rest,
And bid me hence." But, lo! a moment more
The bolts were drawn, and arms whose very touch

Was life, lifted and clasped and bore me in.
"O ghost or angel of my buried love,
I know not, care not which, be welcome here!
Welcome, thrice welcome, to this heart of mine!"
I heard him say, and then I heard no more.

It was high noontide when I woke again,
To hear fierce voices wrangling by my bed, —
My father's and my husband's; for, with dawn,
Gathering up valor, they had sought the tomb,
Had found me gone, and tracked my bleeding feet
Over the pavement to Antonio's door.
Dead, they cared nothing; living, I was theirs.
Hot raged the quarrel; then came Justice in,
And to the court we swept — I in my shroud —
To try the cause.

This was the verdict given:
"A woman who has been to burial borne,
Made fast and left and locked in with the dead;
Who at her husband's door has stood and plead
For entrance, and has heard her prayer denied;
Who from her father's house is urged and chased,
Must be adjudged as dead in law and fact.

The Court pronounces the defendant — dead !
She can resume her former ties at will,
Or may renounce them, if such be her will.
She is no more a daughter, or a spouse,
Unless she choose, and is set free to form
New ties, if so she choose."

O, blessed words !
That very day we knelt before the priest,
My love and I, were wed, and life began.

Child of my child, child of Antonio's child,
Bend down and let me kiss your wondering face.
'T is a strange tale to tell a rose like you.
But time is brief, and, had I told you not,
Haply the story would have met your ears
From them, the Amieri, my own blood,
Now turned to gall, whose foul and bitter lips
Will wag with lies when once my lips are dumb.
(Pardon me, Virgin. I was gentle once,
And thou hast seen my wrongs. Thou wilt forgive.)
Now go, my dearest. When they wake thee up,
To tell thee I am dead, be not too sad.
I, who have died once, do not fear to die.

Sweet was that waking, sweeter will be this.
Close to Heaven's gate my own Antonio sits
Waiting, and, spite of all the Frati say,
I know I shall not stand long at that gate,
Or knock and be refused an entrance there,
For he will start up when he hears my voice,
The saints will smile, and he will open quick.
Only a night to part me from that joy.
Jesu Maria! let the dawning come.

EASTER LILIES.

DARLINGS of June and brides of summer sun,
Chill pipes the stormy wind, the skies are drear ;
Dull and despoiled the gardens every one :
What do you here ?

We looked to see your gracious blooms arise
Mid soft and wooing airs in gardens green,
Where venturesome brown bees and butterflies
Should hail you queen.

Here is no bee nor glancing butterfly ;
They fled on rapid wings before the snow :
Your sister lilies laid them down to die,
Long, long ago.

And here, amid the slowly dropping rain,
We keep our Easter feast, with hearts whose care
Mars the high cadence of each lofty strain,
Each thankful prayer.

But not a shadow dims your joyance sweet,
No baffled hope or memory darkly clad ;
You lay your whiteness at the Lord's dear feet,
And are all glad.

O coward soul ! arouse thee and draw near,
Led by these fragrant acolytes to-day !
Let their sweet confidence rebuke thy fear,
Thy cold delay.

Come with thy darkness to the healing light,
Come with thy bitter, which shall be made sweet,
And lay thy soil beside the lilies white,
At His dear feet !

EBB-TIDE.

LONG reaches of wet grasses sway
Where ran the sea but yesterday,
And white-winged boats at sunset drew
To anchor in the crimsoning blue.
The boats lie on the grassy plain,
Nor tug nor fret at anchor chain ;
Their errand done, their impulse spent,
Chained by an alien element,
With sails unset they idly lie,
Though morning beckons brave and nigh ;
Like wounded birds, their flight denied,
They lie, and long and wait the tide.

About their keels, within the net
Of tough grass fibres green and wet,
A myriad thirsty creatures, pent
In sorrowful imprisonment,
Await the beat, distinct and sweet,
Of the white waves' returning feet.

My soul their vigil joins, and shares
A nobler discontent than theirs;
Athirst like them, I patiently
Sit listening beside the sea,
And still the waters outward glide:
When is the turning of the tide?

Come, pulse of God; come, heavenly thrill!
We wait thy coming, — and we will.
The world is vast, and very far
Its utmost verge and boundaries are;
But thou hast kept thy word to-day
In India and in dim Cathay,
And the same mighty care shall reach
Each humblest rock-pool of this beach.
The gasping fish, the stranded keel,
This dull dry soul of mine, shall feel
Thy freshening touch, and, satisfied,
Shall drink the fulness of the tide.

FLOOD-TIDE.

ALL night the thirsty beach has listening lain,
With patience dumb,
Counting the slow, sad moments of her pain;
Now morn has come,
And with the morn the punctual tide again.

I hear the white battalions down the bay
Charge with a cheer;
The sun's gold lances prick them on their way, —
They plunge, they rear, —
Foam-plumed and snowy-pennoned, they are here!

The rousèd shore, her bright hair backward blown,
Stands on the verge
And waves a smiling welcome, beckoning on
The flying surge,
While round her feet, like doves, the billows crowd and
urge.

Her glad lips quaff the salt, familiar wine ;
Her spent urns fill ;
All hungering creatures know the sound, the sign, —
Quiver and thrill,
With glad expectance crowd and banquet at their will.

I, too, the rapt contentment join and share ;
My tide is full ;
There is new happiness in earth, in air :
All beautiful
And fresh the world but now so bare and dull.

But while we raise the cup of bliss so high,
Thus satisfied,
Another shore beneath a sad, far sky
Waiteth her tide,
And thirsts with sad complainings still denied.

On earth's remotest bound she sits and waits
In doubt and pain ;
Our joy is signal for her sad estates ;
Like dull refrain
Marring our song, her sighings rise in vain.

To each his turn — the ebb-tide and the flood,
The less, the more —
God metes his portions justly out, I know;
But still before
My mind forever floats that pale and grieving shore.

A YEAR.

SHE has been just a year in Heaven.
Unmarked by white moon or gold sun,
By stroke of clock or clang of bell,
Or shadow lengthening on the way,
In the full noon and perfect day,
In Safety's very citadel,
The happy hours have sped, have run;
And, rapt in peace, all pain forgot,
She whom we love, her white soul shriven,
Smiles at the thought and wonders not.

We have been just a year alone, —
A year whose calendar is sighs,
And dull, perpetual wishfulness,
And smiles, each covert for a tear,
And wandering thoughts, half there, half here,
And weariful attempts to guess
The secret of the hiding skies,
The soft, inexorable blue,

With gleaming hints of glory sown,
And Heaven behind, just shining through.

So sweet, so sad, so swift, so slow,
So full of eager growth and light,
So full of pain which blindly grows,
So full of thoughts which either way
Have passed and crossed and touched each day,
To us a thorn, to her a rose;
The year so black, the year so white,
Like rivers twain their course have run;
The earthly stream we trace and know,
But who shall paint the heavenly one?

A year! We gather up our powers,
Our lamps we consecrate and trim;
Open all windows to the day,
And welcome every heavenly air.
We will press forward and will bear,
Having this word to cheer the way:
She, storm-tossed once, is safe with Him,
Healed, comforted, content, forgiven;
And while we count these heavy hours
Has been a year, — a year in Heaven.

TOKENS.

EACH day upon the yellow Nile, 't is said,
Joseph, the youthful ruler, cast forth wheat,
That haply, floating to his father's feet, —
The sad old father, who believed him dead, —
It might be sign in Egypt there was bread;
And thus the patriarch, past the desert sands
And scant oasis fringed with thirsty green,
Be lured toward the love that yearned unseen.
So, flung and scattered — ah! by what dear hands?—
On the swift-rushing and invisible tide,
Small tokens drift adown from far, fair lands,
And say to us, who in the desert bide,
"Are you athirst? Are there no sheaves to bind?
Beloved, here is fulness; follow on and find."

HER GOING.

SUGGESTED BY A PICTURE.

SHE stood in the open door,
She blessed them faint and low:
"I must go," she said, "must go
Away from the light of the sun,
Away from you, every one;
Must see your eyes no more, —
Your eyes, that love me so.

"I should not shudder thus,
Nor weep, nor be afraid,
Nor cling to you so dismayed,
Could I only pierce with my eyes
Where the dark, dark shadow lies;
Where something hideous
Is hiding, perhaps," she said.

Then slowly she went from them,
Went down the staircase grim,

With trembling heart and limb;
Her footfalls echoéd
In the silence vast and dead,
Like the notes of a requiem,
Not sung, but utteréd.

For a little way and a black
She groped as grope the blind,
Then a sudden radiance shined,
And a vision her eyelids burned;
All joyfully she turned,
For a moment turned she back,
And smiled at those behind.

There in the shadows drear
An angel sat serene,
Of grave and tender mien,
With whitest roses crowned;
A scythe lay on the ground,
As reaping-time were near, —
A burnished scythe and a keen.

She did not start or pale
As the angel rose and laid

His hand on hers, nor said
A word, but beckoned on;
For a glorious meaning shone
On the lips that told no tale,
And she followed him, unafraid.

Her friends wept for a space;
Then one said: "Be content;
Surely some good is meant
For her, our Beautiful, —
Some glorious good and full.
Did you not see her face,
Her dear smile, as she went?"

A LONELY MOMENT.

SIT alone in the gray,
The snow falls thick and fast,
And never a sound have I heard all day
But the wailing of the blast,
And the hiss and click of the snow, whirling to and fro.

There seems no living thing
Left in the world but I;
My thoughts fly forth on restless wing,
And drift back wearily,
Storm-beaten, buffeted, hopeless, and almost dead.

No one there is to care;
Not one to even know
Of the lonely day and the dull despair
As the hours ebb and flow,
Slow lingering, as fain to lengthen out my pain.

And I think of the monks of old,
 Each in his separate cell,
Hearing no sound, except when tolled
 The stated convent bell.
How could they live and bear that silence everywhere?

And I think of tumbling seas,
 'Neath cruel, lonely skies;
And shipwrecked sailors over these
 Stretching their hungry eyes, —
Eyes dimmed with wasting tears for weary years on years, —

Pacing the hopeless sand,
 Wistful and wan and pale,
Each foam-flash like a beckoning hand,
 Each wave a glancing sail,
And so for days and days, and still the sail delays.

I hide my eyes in vain,
 In vain I try to smile;
That urging vision comes again,
 The sailor on his isle,
With none to hear his cry, to help him live — or die!

And with the pang a thought
Breaks o'er me like the sun,
Of the great listening Love which caught
Those accents every one,
Nor lost one faintest word, but always, always heard.

The monk his vigil pale
Could lighten with a smile,
The sailor's courage need not fail
Upon his lonely isle;
For there, as here, by sea or land, the pitying Lord stood close at hand.

O coward heart of mine!
When storms shall beat again,
Hold firmly to this thought divine,
As anchorage in pain:
That, lonely though thou seemest to be, the Lord is near, remembering thee.

COMMUNION.

HAT is it to commune?
It is when soul meets soul, and they embrace
As souls may, stooping from each separate sphere
For a brief moment's space.

What is it to commune?
It is to lay the veil of custom by,
To be all unafraid of truth to talk,
Face to face, eye to eye.

Not face to face, dear Lord;
That is the joy of brighter worlds to be;
And yet, Thy bidden guests about Thy board,
We do commune with Thee.

Behind the white-robed priest
Our eyes, anointed with a sudden grace,
Dare to conjecture of a mighty guest,
A dim belovéd Face.

And is it Thou, indeed?
And dost Thou lay Thy glory all away
To visit us, and with Thy grace to feed
Our hungering hearts to-day?

And can a thing so sweet,
And can such heavenly condescension be?
Ah! wherefore tarry thus our lingering feet?
It can be none but Thee.

There is the gracious ear
That never yet was deaf to sinner's call;
We will not linger, and we dare not fear,
But kneel, — and tell Thee all.

We tell Thee of our sin
Only half loathed, only half wished away,
And those clear eyes of Love that look within
Rebuke us, seem to say, —

"O, bought with my own blood,
Mine own, for whom my precious life I gave,
Am I so little prized, remembered, loved,
By those I died to save?"

And under that deep gaze
Sorrow awakes ; we kneel with eyelids wet,
And marvel, as with Peter at the gate,
That we could so forget.

We tell Thee of our care,
Of the sore burden, pressing day by day,
And in the light and pity of Thy face
The burden melts away.

We breathe our secret wish,
The importunate longing which no man may see ;
We ask it humbly, or, more restful still,
We leave it all to Thee.

And last our amulet
Of precious names we thread, and soft and low
We crave for each beloved, or near or far,
A blessing ere we go.

The thorns are turned to flowers,
All dark perplexities seem light and fair,
A mist is lifted from the heavy hours,
And Thou art everywhere.

A FAREWELL.

GO, sun, since go you must,
The dusky evening lowers above our sky,
Our sky which was so blue and sweetly fair;
Night is not terrible that we should sigh.
A little darkness we can surely bear;
Will there not be more sunshine — by and by?

Go, rose, since go you must,
Flowerless and chill the winter draweth nigh;
Closed are the blithe and fragrant lips which made
All summer long perpetual melody.
Cheerless we take our way, but not afraid:
Will there not be more roses — by and by?

Go, love, since go you must,
Out of our pain we bless you as you fly;
The momentary heaven the rainbow lit
Was worth whole days of black and stormy sky;
Shall we not see, as by the waves we sit,
Your bright sail winging shoreward — by and by?

Go, life, since go you must,
Uncertain guest and whimsical ally !
All questionless you came, unquestioned go ;
What does it mean to live, or what to die ?
Smiling we watch you vanish, for we know
Somewhere is nobler living — by and by.

EBB AND FLOW.

HOW easily He turns the tides !
Just now the yellow beach was dry,
Just now the gaunt rocks all were bare,
The sun beat hot, and thirstily
Each sea-weed waved its long brown hair,
And bent and languished as in pain ;
Then, in a flashing moment's space,
The white foam-feet which spurned the sand
Paused in their joyous outward race,
Wheeled, wavered, turned them to the land,
And, a swift legionary band,
Poured on the waiting shores again.

How easily He turns the tides !
The fulness of my yesterday
Has vanished like a rapid dream,
And pitiless and far away
The cool, refreshing waters gleam :
Grim rocks of dread and doubt and pain

Rear their dark fronts where once was sea ;
  But I can smile and wait for Him
Who turns the tides so easily,
  Fills the spent rock-pool to its brim,
And up from the horizon dim
  Leads His bright morning waves again.

ANGELUS.

SOFTLY drops the crimson sun :
Softly down from overhead,
Drop the bell-notes, one by one,
Melting in the melting red ;
Sign to angel bands unsleeping, —
" Day is done, the dark is dread,
Take the world in care and keeping.

" Set the white-robed sentries close,
Wrap our want and weariness
In the surety of repose ;
Let the shining presences,
Bearing fragrance on their wings,
Stand about our beds to bless,
Fright away all evil things.

"Rays of Him whose shadow pours
Through all lives a brimming glory,
Float o'er darksome woods and moors,
Float above the billows hoary;
Shine, through night and storm and sin,
Tangled fate and bitter story,
Guide the lost and wandering in!"

Now the last red ray is gone;
Now the twilight shadows hie;
Still the bell-notes, one by one,
Send their soft voice to the sky,
Praying, as with human lip, —
"Angels, hasten, night is nigh,
Take us to thy guardianship."

THE MORNING COMES BEFORE THE SUN.

SLOW buds the pink dawn like a rose
From out night's gray and cloudy sheath;
Softly and still it grows and grows,
Petal by petal, leaf by leaf;
Each sleep-imprisoned creature breaks
Its dreamy fetters, one by one,
And love awakes, and labor wakes, —
The morning comes before the sun.

What is this message from the light
So fairer far than light can be?
Youth stands a-tiptoe, eager, bright,
In haste the risen sun to see;
Ah! check thy longing, restless heart,
Count the charmed moments as they run,
It is life's best and fairest part,
This morning hour before the sun.

When once thy day shall burst to flower,
  When once the sun shall climb the sky,
And busy hour by busy hour,
  The urgent noontide draws anigh ;
When the long shadows creep abreast,
  To dim the happy task half done,
Thou wilt recall this pause of rest,
  This morning hush before the sun.

To each, one dawning and one dew,
  One fresh young hour is given by fate,
One rose flush on the early blue.
  Be not impatient then, but wait !
Clasp the sweet peace on earth and sky,
  By midnight angels woven and spun ;
Better than day its prophecy, —
  The morning comes before the sun.

LABORARE EST ORARE.

"Although St. Francesca was unwearied in her devotions, yet if, during her prayers, she was called away by her husband or any domestic duty, she would close the book cheerfully, saying that a wife and a mother, when called upon, must quit her God at the altar to find Him in her domestic affairs." — *Legends of the Monastic Orders.*

HOW infinite and sweet, Thou everywhere
  And all abounding Love, Thy service is !
Thou liest an ocean round my world of care,
My petty every-day ; and fresh and fair,
  Pour Thy strong tides through all my crevices,
Until the silence ripples into prayer.

That Thy full glory may abound, increase,
  And so Thy likeness shall be formed in me,
I pray ; the answer is not rest or peace,
But charges, duties, wants, anxieties,
  Till there seems room for everything but Thee,
And never time for anything but these.

And I should fear, but lo ! amid the press,
  The whirl and hum and pressure of my day,

I hear Thy garment's sweep, Thy seamless dress,
And close beside my work and weariness
  Discern Thy gracious form, not far away,
But very near, O Lord, to help and bless.

The busy fingers fly, the eyes may see
  Only the glancing needle which they hold,
But all my life is blossoming inwardly,
And every breath is like a litany,
  While through each labor, like a thread of gold,
Is woven the sweet consciousness of Thee.

EIGHTEEN.

AH! grown a dim and fairy shade,
Dear child, who, fifteen years ago,
Out of our arms escaped and fled
With swift white feet, as if afraid,
To hide beneath the grass, the snow,
That sunny little head.

This is your birthday! Fair, so fair,
And grown to gracious maiden-height,
And versed in heavenly lore and ways;
White-vested as the angels are,
In very light of very light,
Somehow, somewhere, you keep the day

With those new friends, whom "new" we call,
But who are dearer now than we,
And better known by face and name:
And do they smile and say, "How tall
The child becomes, how radiant, she
Who was so little when she came!"

Darling, we count your eighteen years, —
Fifteen in Heaven, on earth but three, —
And try to frame you grown and wise :
But all in vain ; there still appears
Only the child you used to be,
Our baby with the violet eyes.

OUTWARD BOUND.

A GRIEVOUS day of wrathful winds,
Of low-hung clouds, which scud and fly,
And drop cold rains, then lift and show
A sullen realm of upper sky.

The sea is black as night; it roars
From lips afoam with cruel spray,
Like some fierce, many-throated pack
Of wolves, which scents and chases prey.

Crouched in my little wind-swept nook,
I hear the menacing voices call,
And shudder, as above the deck
Topples and swings the weltering wall.

It seems a vast and restless grave,
Insatiate, hungry, beckoning
With dreadful gesture of command
To every free and living thing.

"O Lord," I cry, "Thou makest life
 And hope and all sweet things to be;
Rebuke this hovering, following Death, —
 This horror never born of Thee."

A sudden gleam, the waves light up
 With radiant, momentary hues, —
Amber and shadowy pearl and gold,
 Opal and green and unknown blues, —

And, rising on the tossing walls,
 Within the foaming valleys swung,
Soft shapes of sea-birds, dimly seen,
 Flutter and float and call their young,

A moment; then the lowering clouds
 Settle anew above the main,
The colors die, the waves rise higher,
 And night and terror rule again.

No more I see the small, dim shapes,
 So unafraid of wind and wave,
Nestling beneath the tempest's roar,
 Cradled in what I deemed a grave.

But all night long I lay and smiled
  At thought of those soft folded wings,
And trusting, with the trustful birds,
  In Him who cares for smallest things.

FROM EAST TO WEST.

THE boat cast loose her moorings;
"Good-by" was all we said.
"Good-by, Old World," we said with a smile,
And never looked back as we sped,
A shining wake of foam behind,
To the heart of the sunset red.

Heavily drove our plunging keel
The warring waves between;
Heavily strove we night and day,
Against the west-wind keen,
Bent, like a foe, to bar our path, —
A foe with an awful mien.

Never a token met our eyes
From the dear land far away;
No storm-swept bird, no drifting branch,
To tell us where it lay.

Wearily searched we, hour by hour,
Through the mist and the driving spray,

Till, all in a flashing moment,
The fog-veils rent and flew,
And a blithesome south-wind caught the sails
And whistled the cordage through,
And the stars swung low their silver lamps
In a dome of airy blue,

And, breathed from unseen distances,
A new and joyous air
Caressed our senses suddenly
With a rapture fresh and rare.
"It is the breath of home!" we cried;
"We feel that we are there."

O Land whose tent-roof is the dome
Of Heaven's purest sky,
Whose mighty heart inspires the wind
Of glad, strong liberty,
Standing upon thy sunset shore,
Beside the waters high,

Long may thy rosy smile be bright;
  Above the ocean din
Thy young, undaunted voice be heard,
  Calling the whole world kin;
And ever be thy arms held out
  To take the storm-tossed in!

UNA.

MY darling once lived by my side,
She scarcely ever went away;
We shared our studies and our play,
Nor did she care to walk or ride
Unless I did the same that day.

Now she is gone to some far place;
I never see her any more,
The pleasant play-times all are o'er;
I come from school, there is no face
To greet me at the open door.

At first I cried all day, all night;
I could not bear to eat or smile,
I missed her, missed her, all the while;
The brightest day did not look bright,
The shortest walk was like a mile.

Then some one came and told me this :
  "Your playmate is but gone from view,
  Close by your side she stands, and you
Can almost hear her breathe, and kiss
  Her soft cheek as you used to do.

"Only a little veil between, —
  A slight, thin veil ; if you could see
  Past its gray folds, there she would be,
Smiling and sweet, and she would lean
  And stretch her hands out joyfully.

"All the day long, and year by year,
  She will go forward as you go ;
  As you grow older, she will grow ;
As you grow good, she, with her clear
  And angel eyes, will mark and know.

"Think, when you wake up every day,
  That she is standing by your bed,
  Close to the pillow where her head,
Her little curly head, once lay,
  With a 'Good-morning' smiled, not said.

"Think, when the books seem dull and tame,
  The sports no longer what they were,
  That there she sits, a shape of air,
And turns the leaf or joins the game
  With the same smile she used to wear.

"So, moving on still, hand in hand,
  One of these days your eyes will clear,
  The hiding veil will disappear,
And you will know and understand
  Just why your playmate left you here."

This made me happier, and I try
  To think each day that it may be.
  Sometimes I do so easily;
But then again I have to cry,
  Because I want so much to *see!*

TWO WAYS TO LOVE.

"Entre deux amants il y a toujours l'un qui baise et l'autre qui tend la joue."

I.

HE says he loves me well, and I
  Believe it; in my hands, to make
Or mar, his life lies utterly,
Nor can I the strong plea deny,
  Which claims my love for his love's sake.

He says there is no face so fair
  As mine; when I draw near, his eyes
Light up; each ripple of my hair
He loves; the very cloak I wear
  He touches fondly where it lies.

And roses, roses all the way,
  Upon my path fall, strewed by him;
His tenderness by night, by day,
Keeps faithful watch to heap alway
  My cup of pleasure to the brim.

The other women, full of spite,
  Count me the happiest woman born
To be so worshipped ; I delight
To flaunt his homage in their sight, —
  For me the rose, for them its thorn.

I love him, — or I think I do ;
  Sure one *must* love what is so sweet.
He is all tender and all true,
All eloquent to plead and sue,
  All strength — though kneeling at my feet.

Yet I had visions once of yore,
  Girlish imaginings of a zest,
A possible thrill, — but why run o'er
These fancies? — idle dreams, no more ;
  I will forget them, this is best.

So let him take, — the past is past ;
  The future, with its golden key,
Into his outstretched hands I cast.
I shall love him — perhaps — at last,
  As now I love his love for me.

II.

Not as all other women may,
  Love I my Love; he is so great,
So beautiful, I dare essay
No nearness, but in silence lay
  My heart upon his path, — and wait.

Poor heart! its beatings are so low
  He does not heed them passing by,
Save as one heeds, where violets grow,
A fragrance, caring not to know
  Where the veiled purple buds may lie.

I sometimes think that it is dead,
  It lies so still. I bend and lean,
Like mother over cradle-head,
Wondering if still faint breaths are shed
  Like sighs the parted lips between.

And then, with vivid pulse and thrill,
It quickens into sudden bliss
At sound of step or voice, nor will
Be hushed, although, regardless still,
He knows not, cares not, it is his.

I would not lift it if I could :
The little flame, though faint and dim
As glow-worm spark in lonely wood,
Shining where no man calls it good,
May one day light the path for him, —

May guide his way, or soon or late,
Through blinding mist or wintry rain ;
And, so content, I watch and wait.
Let others share his happier fate,
I only ask to share his pain !

And if some day, when passing by,
My dear Love should his steps arrest,
Should mark the poor heart waiting nigh,
Should know it his, should lift it, — why,
Patience is good, but joy is best !

AFTER-GLOW.

Y morn was all dewy rose and pearl,
  Peace brimmed the skies, a cool and fragrant air
  Caressed my going forth, and everywhere
The radiant webs, by hope and fancy spun,
    Stretched shining in the sun.

Then came a noon, hot, breathless, still, —
  No wind to visit the dew-thirsty flowers,
  Only the dust, the road, the urging hours;
And, pressing on, I never guessed or knew
    That day was half-way through.

And when the pomp of purple lit the sky,
  And sheaves of golden lances tipped with red
  Danced in the west, wondering I gazed, and said,
"Lo, a new morning comes, my hopes to crown!"
    Sudden the sun dropped down

Like a great golden ball into the sea,
  Which made room, laughing, and the serried rank
  Of yellow lances flashed, and, turning, sank
After their chieftain, as he led the way,
    And all the heaven was gray.

Startled and pale, I stood to see them go ;
  Then a long, stealing shadow to me crept,
  And laid his cold hand on me, and I wept
And hid my eyes, and shivered with affright
    At thought of coming night.

But as I wept and shuddered, a warm thrill
  Smote on my sense. I raised my eyes, and lo !
  The skies, so dim but now, were all aglow
With a new flush of tender rose and gold,
    Opening fold on fold.

Higher and higher soared the gracious beam,
  Deeper and deeper glowed the heavenly hues,
  Nor any cowering shadow could refuse
The beautiful embrace which clasped and kissed
    Its dun to amethyst.

A little longer, and the lovely light,
  Draining the last drops from its wondrous urn,
  Departed, and the swart shades in their turn,
Impatient of the momentary mirth,
    Crowded to seize the earth.

No longer do I shudder. With calm eye
  I front the night, nor wish its hours away;
  For in that message from my banished day
I read his pledge of dawn, and soon or late
    I can endure to wait.

HOPE AND I.

HOPE stood one morning by the way,
And stretched her fair right hand to me,
And softly whispered, "For this day
I 'll company with thee."

"Ah, no, dear Hope," I sighing said;
"Oft have you joined me in the morn,
But when the evening came, you fled
And left me all forlorn.

"'T is better I should walk alone
Than have your company awhile,
And then to lose it, and go on
For weary mile on mile."

She turned, rebuked. I went my way,
But sad the sunshine seemed, and chill;
I missed her, missed her all the day,
And O, I miss her still.

LEFT BEHIND.

WE started in the morning, a morning full of glee,
All in the early morning, a goodly company;
And some were full of merriment, and all were kind and dear;
But the others have pursued their way, and left me sitting here.

My feet were not so fleet as theirs, my courage soon was gone,
And so I lagged and fell behind, although they cried "Come on!"
They cheered me and they pitied me, but one by one went by,
For the stronger must outstrip the weak: there is no remedy.

Some never looked behind, but smiled, and swiftly, hand
in hand,
Departed with a strange sweet joy I could not understand;
I know not by what silver streams their roses bud and
blow,
But I am glad — O very glad — they should be happy so.

And some they went companionless, yet not alone, it
seemed,
For there were sounds of rustling wings, and songs, — or
else we dreamed;
And a glow from lights invisible to us lit up the place,
And tinged, as if with glory, each dear and parting face.

So happy, happy did they look, as one by one they went,
That we, who missed them sorely, were fain to be content;
And I, who sit the last of all, left far behind, alone,
Cannot be sorry for their sakes, but only for my own.

My eyes seek out the different paths by which they went
away,
And oft I wish to follow, but oftener wish to stay;
For fair as may the new things be, the farther things they
know,
This is a pleasant resting-place, a pleasant place also.

There are flowers for the gathering, which grow my path
anear,
The skies are fair, and everywhere the sun is warm and
clear:
I may have missed the wine of life, the strong wine and
the new,
But I have my wells of water, my sips of honey-dew.

So when I turn my thoughts from those who shared my
dawn of day,
My fresh and joyous morning prime, and now are passed
away,
I can see just how sweet all is, how good, and be resigned
To sit thus in the afternoon, alone and left behind.

SAVOIR C'EST PARDONNER.

MYRIAD rivers seek the sea,
The sea rejects not any one ;
A myriad rays of light may be
Clasped in the compass of one sun ;
And myriad grasses, wild and free,
Drink of the dew which faileth none.

A myriad worlds encompass ours ;
A myriad souls our souls enclose ;
And each, its sins and woes and powers,
The Lord He sees, the Lord He knows,
And from the Infinite Knowledge flowers
The Infinite Pity's fadeless rose.

Lighten our darkness, Lord, most wise ;
All-seeing One, give us to see ;
Our judgments are profanities,
Our ignorance is cruelty,
While Thou, knowing all, dost not despise
To pardon even such things as we.

MORNING.

O WORD and thing most beautiful!
Our yesterday was cold and dull,
Gray mists obscured the setting sun,
Its evening wept with sobbing rain;
But to and fro, mid shrouding night,
Some healing angel swift has run,
And all is fresh and fair again.

O, word and thing most beautiful!
The hearts, which were of cares so full,
The tired hands, the tired feet,
So glad of night, are glad of morn, —
Where are the clouds of yesterday?
The world is good, the world is sweet,
And life is new and hope re-born.

O, word and thing most beautiful !
O coward soul and sorrowful,
  Which sighs to note the ebbing light
Give place to evening's shadowy gray !
  What are these things but parables, —
That darkness heals the wrongs of day,
  And dawning clears all mists of night.

O, word and thing most beautiful !
The little sleep our cares to lull,
  The long, soft dusk and then sunrise,
To waken fresh and angel fair,
  Life all renewed and cares forgot,
  Ready for Heaven's glad surprise,
So Christ, who is our Light, be there.

A BLIND SINGER.

N covert of a leafy porch,
Where woodbine clings,
And roses drop their crimson leaves,
He sits and sings;
With soft brown crest erect to hear,
And drooping wings.

Shut in a narrow cage, which bars
His eager flight,
Shut in the darker prison-house
Of blinded sight,
Alike to him are sun and stars,
The day, the night.

But all the fervor of high noon,
Hushed, fragrant, strong,

And all the peace of moonlit nights
When nights are long,
And all the bliss of summer eves,
Breathe in his song.

The rustle of the fresh green woods,
The hum of bee,
The joy of flight, the perfumed waft
Of blossoming tree,
The half-forgotten, rapturous thrill
Of liberty, —

All blend and mix, while evermore,
Now and again,
A plaintive, puzzled cadence comes,
A low refrain,
Caught from some shadowy memory
Of patient pain.

In midnight black, when all men sleep,
My singer wakes,
And pipes his lovely melodies,
And trills and shakes.
The dark sky bends to listen, but
No answer makes.

O, what is joy? In vain we grasp
    Her purple wings;
Unwon, unwooed, she flits to dwell
    With humble things;
She shares my sightless singer's cage,
    And so — he sings.

MARY.

HE drowsy summer in the flowering limes
Had laid her down at ease,
Lulled by soft, sportive winds, whose tinkling chimes
Summoned the wandering bees
To feast, and dance, and hold high carnival
Within that vast and fragrant banquet-hall.

She stood, my Mary, on the wall below,
Poised on light, arching feet,
And drew the long, green branches down to show
Where hung, mid odors sweet, —
A tiny miracle to touch and view, —
The humming-bird's small nest and pearls of blue.

Fair as the summer's self she stood, and smiled,
With eyes like summer sky,

Wistful and glad, half-matron and half-child,
Gentle and proud and shy;
Her sweet head framed against the blossoming bough,
She stood a moment, — and she stands there now!

'T is sixteen years since, trustful, unafraid,
In her full noon of light,
She passed beneath the grass's curtaining shade,
Out of our mortal sight;
And springs and summers, bearing gifts to men,
And long, long winters have gone by since then.

And each some little gift has brought to dress
That unforgotten bed, —
Violet, anemone, or lady's-tress,
Or spray of berries red,
Or purpling leaf, or mantle, pure and cold,
Of winnowed snow, wrapped round it, fold on fold.

Yet still she stands, a glad and radiant shape,
Set in the morning fair, —
That vanished morn which had such swift escape.
I turn and see her there, —
The arch, sweet smile, the bending, graceful head;
And, seeing thus, why do I call her dead?

WHEN LOVE WENT.

HAT whispered Love the day he fled?
Ah! this was what Love whispered:
"You sought to hold me with a chain;
I fly to prove such holding vain.

"You bound me burdens, and I bore
The burdens hard, the burdens sore;
I bore them all unmurmuring,
For Love can bear a harder thing.

"You taxed me often, teased me, wept;
I only smiled, and still I kept
Through storm and sun and night and day,
My joyous, viewless, faithful way.

"But, dear, once dearest, you and I
This day have parted company.
Love must be free to give, defer,
Himself alone his almoner.

"As free I freely poured my all,
Enslaved I spurn, renounce my thrall,
Its wages and its bitter bread."
Thus whispered Love the day he fled!

OVERSHADOWED.

"Insomuch that they brought forth the sick into the streets, and laid them on beds and couches, that at the least the shadow of Peter, passing by, might overshadow some of them."

ID the thronged bustle of the city street,
In the hot hush of noon,
I wait, with folded hands and nerveless feet.
Surely He will come soon.
Surely the Healer will not pass me by,
But listen to my cry.

Long are the hours in which I lie and wait,
Heavy the load I bear ;
But He will come ere evening. Soon or late
I shall behold Him there ;
Shall hear His dear voice, all the clangor through :
"What wilt thou that I do ?"

"If Thou but wilt, Lord, Thou canst make me clean."
Thus shall I answer swift.

And He will touch me, as He walks serene;
  And I shall rise and lift
This couch, so long my prison-house of pain,
And be made whole again.

He lingers yet. But lo! a hush, a hum.
  The multitudes press on
After some leader. Surely He is come!
  He nears me; He is gone!
Only His shadow reached me, as He went;
Yet here I rest content.

In that dear shadow, like some healing spell,
  A heavenly patience lay;
Its balm of peace enwrapped me as it fell;
  My pains all fled away,—
The weariness, the deep unrest of soul;
I am indeed "made whole."

It is enough, Lord, though Thy face divine
  Was turned to other men.
Although no touch, no questioning voice was mine,
  Thou wilt come once again;
And, if Thy shadow brings such bliss to me,
What must Thy presence be?

TIME TO GO.

THEY know the time to go!
The fairy clocks strike their inaudible hour
In field and woodland, and each punctual flower
Bows at the signal an obedient head
And hastes to bed.

The pale Anemone
Glides on her way with scarcely a good-night;
The Violets tie their purple nightcaps tight;
Hand clasped in hand, the dancing Columbines,
In blithesome lines,

Drop their last courtesies,
Flit from the scene, and couch them for their rest;
The Meadow Lily folds her scarlet vest
And hides it 'neath the Grasses' lengthening green;
Fair and serene,

Her sister Lily floats
On the blue pond, and raises golden eyes
To court the golden splendor of the skies, —
The sudden signal comes, and down she goes
To find repose

In the cool depths below.
A little later, and the Asters blue
Depart in crowds, a brave and cheery crew;
While Golden-rod, still wide awake and gay,
Turns him away,

Furls his bright parasol,
And, like a little hero, meets his fate.
The Gentians, very proud to sit up late,
Next follow. Every Fern is tucked and set
'Neath coverlet,

Downy and soft and warm.
No little seedling voice is heard to grieve
Or make complaints the folding woods beneath;
No lingerer dares to stay, for well they know
The time to go.

Teach us your patience, brave,
Dear flowers, till we shall dare to part like you,
Willing God's will, sure that his clock strikes true,
That his sweet day augurs a sweeter morrow,
With smiles, not sorrow.

GULF-STREAM.

ONELY and cold and fierce I keep my way,
Scourge of the lands, companioned by the storm,
Tossing to heaven my frontlet, wild and gray,
Mateless, yet conscious ever of a warm
And brooding presence close to mine all day.

What is this alien thing, so near, so far,
Close to my life always, but blending never?
Hemmed in by walls whose crystal gates unbar
Not at the instance of my strong endeavor
To pierce the stronghold where their secrets are?

Buoyant, impalpable, relentless, thin,
Rise the clear, mocking walls. I strive in vain
To reach the pulsing heart that beats within,
Or with persistence of a cold disdain,
To quell the gladness which I may not win.

Forever sundered and forever one,
  Linked by a bond whose spell I may not guess,
Our hostile, yet embracing currents run ;
  Such wedlock lonelier is than loneliness.
Baffled, withheld, I clasp the bride I shun.

Yet even in my wrath a wild regret
  Mingles ; a bitterness of jealous strife
Tinges my fury as I foam and fret
  Against the borders of that calmer life,
Beside whose course my wrathful course is set.

But all my anger, all my pain and woe,
  Are vain to daunt her gladness ; all the while
She goes rejoicing, and I do not know,
  Catching the soft irradiance of her smile,
If I am most her lover or her foe.

MY WHITE CHRYSANTHEMUM.

AS purely white as is the drifted snow,
More dazzling fair than summer roses are,
Petalled with rays like a clear rounded star,
When winds pipe chilly, and red sunsets glow,
Your blossoms blow.

Sweet with a freshening fragrance, all their own,
In which a faint, dim breath of bitter lies,
Like wholesome breath mid honeyed flatteries;
When other blooms are dead, and birds have flown,
You stand alone.

Fronting the winter with a fearless grace,
Flavoring the odorless gray autumn chill,
Nipped by the furtive frosts, but cheery still,
Lifting to heaven from the bare garden place
A smiling face.

Roses are fair, but frail, and soon grow faint,
  Nor can endure a hardness; violets blue,
  Short-lived and sweet, live but a day or two;
The nun-like lily bows without complaint,
    And dies a saint.

Each following each they hasten them away,
  And leave us to our winter and our rue,
  Sad and uncomforted; you, only you,
Dear, hardy lover, keep your faith and stay
    Long as you may.

And so we choose you out from all the rest,
  For that most noble word of "Loyalty,"
  Which blazoned on your petals seems to be;
Winter is near, — stay with us; be our guest,
    The last and best.

TILL THE DAY DAWN.

WHY should I weary you, dear heart, with words,
Words all discordant with a foolish pain?
Thoughts cannot interrupt or prayers do wrong,
And soft and silent as the summer rain
Mine fall upon your pathway all day long.

Giving as God gives, counting not the cost
Of broken box or spilled and fragrant oil,
I know that, spite of your strong carelessness,
Rest must be sweeter, worthier must be toil,
Touched with such mute, invisible caress.

One of these days, our weary ways quite trod,
Made free at last and unafraid of men,
I shall draw near and reach to you my hand.
And you? Ah! well, we shall be spirits then.
I think you will be glad and understand.

MY BIRTHDAY.

WHO is this who gently slips
 Through my door, and stands and sighs,
Hovering in a soft eclipse,
With a finger on her lips
 And a meaning in her eyes?

Once she came to visit me
 In white robes with festal airs,
Glad surprises, songs of glee;
Now in silence cometh she,
 And a sombre garb she wears.

Once I waited and was tired,
 Chid her visits as too few;
Crownless now and undesired,
She to seek me is inspired
 Oftener than she used to do.

Grave her coming is and still,
  Sober her appealing mien,
Tender thoughts her glances fill;
But I shudder, as one will
  When an open grave is seen.

Wherefore, friend, — for friend thou art, —
  Should I wrong thee thus and grieve?
Wherefore push thee from my heart?
Of my morning thou wert part;
  Be a part too of my eve.

See, I hold my hand to meet
  That cool, shadowy hand of thine;
Hold it firmly, it is sweet
Thus to clasp and thus to greet,
  Though no more in full sunshine.

Come and freely seek my door,
  I will open willingly;
I will chide the past no more,
Looking to the things before,
  Led by pathways known to thee.

BY THE CRADLE.

THE baby Summer lies asleep and dreaming —
Dreaming and blooming like a guarded rose;
And March, a kindly nurse, though rude of seeming,
Is watching by the cradle hung with snows.

Her blowing winds but keep the rockers swinging,
And deepen slumber in the shut blue eyes,
And the shrill cadences of her high singing
Are to the babe but wonted lullabies.

She draws the coverlet white and tucks it trimly,
She folds the little sleeper safe from harm,
Or bends to lift the veil, and, peering inly,
Makes sure it lies all undisturbed and warm.

And so she sits, till in the still, gray dawning
Two fairer nurses come, her place to take,
And smiling, beaming, with no word of warning,
Draw off the quilt, and kiss the babe awake.

A THUNDER STORM.

THE day was hot and the day was dumb,
Save for cricket's chirr or the bee's low hum,
Not a bird was seen or a butterfly,
And ever till noon was over, the sun
Glared down with a yellow and terrible eye;

Glared down in the woods, where the breathless boughs
Hung heavy and faint in a languid drowse,
And the ferns were curling with thirst and heat;
Glared down on the fields where the sleepy cows
Stood munching the grasses, dry and sweet.

Then a single cloud rose up in the west,
With a base of gray and a white, white crest;
It rose and it spread a mighty wing,
And swooped at the sun, though he did his best
And struggled and fought like a wounded thing.

8

And the woods awoke, and the sleepers heard,
Each heavily hanging leaflet stirred
  With a little expectant quiver and thrill,
As the cloud bent over and uttered a word, —
  One volleying, rolling syllable.

And once and again came the deep, low tone
Which only to thunder's lips is known,
  And the earth held up her fearless face
And listened as if to a signal blown, —
  A signal-trump in some heavenly place.

The trumpet of God, obeyed on high,
His signal to open the granary
  And send forth his heavily loaded wains
Rumbling and roaring down the sky
  And scattering the blessed, long-harvested rains.

THROUGH THE DOOR.

THE angel opened the door
A little way,
And she vanished, as melts a star,
Into the day.
And, for just a second's space,
Ere the bar he drew,
The pitying angel paused,
And we looked through.

What did we see within?
Ah! who can tell?
What glory and glow of light
Ineffable;
What peace in the very air,
What hush and calm,
Soothing each tired soul
Like healing balm!

Was it a dream we dreamed,
    Or did we hear
The harping of silver harps,
    Divinely clear?
A murmur of that "new song,"
    Which, soft and low,
The happy angels sing, —
    Sing as they go?

And, as in the legend old,
    The good monk heard,
As he paced his cloister dim,
    A heavenly bird,
And, rapt and lost in the joy
    Of the wondrous song,
Listened a hundred years,
    Nor deemed them long,

So chained in sense and limb,
    All blind with sun,
We stood and tasted the joy
    Of our vanished one;

And we took no note of time,
Till soon or late
The gentle angel sighed,
And shut the gate.

The vision is closed and sealed.
We are come back
To the old, accustomed earth,
The well-worn track, —
Back to the daily toil,
The daily pain, —
But we never can be the same,
Never again.

We who have bathed in noon,
All radiant white,
Shall we come back content
To sit in night?
Content with self and sin,
The stain, the blot?
To have stood so near the gate
And enter not?

O glimpse so swift, so sweet,
So soon withdrawn !
Stay with us ; light our dusks
Till day shall dawn ;
Until the shadows flee,
And to our view
Again the gate unbars,
And we pass through.

READJUSTMENT.

AFTER the earthquake shock or lightning dart
Comes a recoil of silence o'er the lands,
And then, with pulses hot and quivering hands,
Earth calls up courage to her mighty heart,
Plies every tender, compensating art,
Draws her green, flowery veil above the scar,
Fills the shrunk hollow, smooths the riven plain,
And with a century's tendance heals again
The seams and gashes which her fairness mar.
So we, when sudden woe like lightning sped,
Finds us and smites us in our guarded place,
After one brief, bewildered moment's space,
By the same heavenly instinct taught and led,
Adjust our lives to loss, make friends with pain,
Bind all our shattered hopes and bid them bloom again.

AT THE GATE.

"For behold, the kingdom of God is within you."

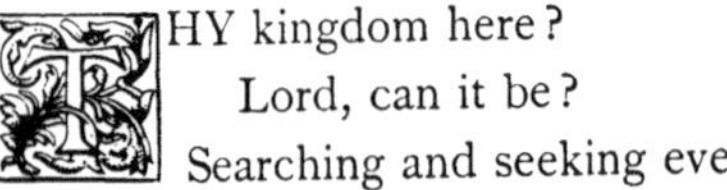

HY kingdom here?
Lord, can it be?
Searching and seeking everywhere
For many a year,
"Thy kingdom come" has been my prayer.
Was that dear kingdom all the while so near?

Blinded and dull
With selfish sin,
Have I been sitting at the gates
Called Beautiful,
Where Thy fair angel stands and waits,
With hand upon the lock to let me in?

Was I the wall
Which barred the way,
Darkening the glory of Thy grace,
Hiding the ray
Which, shining out as from Thy very face,
Had shown to other men the perfect day?

Was I the bar
Which shut me out
From the full joyance which they taste
Whose spirits are
Within Thy Paradise embraced, —
Thy blessed Paradise, which seemed so far?

The vision swells :
I seem to catch
Celestial breezes, rustling low,
The asphodels,
Where, singing softly ever to and fro,
Moves each fair saint who in Thy presence dwells.

Let me not sit
Another hour,
Idly awaiting what is mine to win,
Blinded in wit.
Lord Jesus, rend these walls of self and sin ;
Beat down the gate, that I may enter it.

A HOME.

WHAT is a home? A guarded space,
Wherein a few, unfairly blest,
Shall sit together, face to face,
And bask and purr and be at rest?

Where cushioned walls rise up between
Its inmates and the common air,
The common pain, and pad and screen
From blows of fate or winds of care?

Where Art may blossom strong and free,
And Pleasure furl her silken wing,
And every laden moment be
A precious and peculiar thing?

And Past and Future, softly veiled
In hiding mists, shall float and lie
Forgotten half, and unassailed
By either hope or memory,

While the luxurious Present weaves
  Her perfumed spells untried, untrue,
Broiders her garments, heaps her sheaves,
  All for the pleasure of a few?

Can it be this, the longed-for thing
  Which wanderers on the restless foam,
Unsheltered beggars, birds on wing,
  Aspire to, dream of, christen "Home"?

No. Art may bloom, and peace and bliss;
  Grief may refrain and Death forget;
But if there be no more than this,
  The soul of home is wanting yet.

Dim image from far glory caught,
  Fair type of fairer things to be,
The true home rises in our thought,
  A beacon set for men to see.

Its lamps burn freely in the night,
  Its fire-glows unchidden shed
Their cheering and abounding light
  On homeless folk uncomforted.

Each sweet and secret thing within
  Gives out a fragrance on the air, —
A thankful breath, sent forth to win
  A little smile from others' care.

The few, they bask in closer heat;
  The many catch the further ray.
Life higher seems, the world more sweet,
  And hope and Heaven less far away.

So the old miracle anew
  Is wrought on earth and provéd good,
And crumbs apportioned for a few,
  God-blessed, suffice a multitude.

THE LEGEND OF KINTU.

WHEN earth was young and men were few,
And all things freshly born and new
Seemed made for blessing, not for ban,
Kintu, the god, appeared as man.
Clad in the plain white priestly dress,
He journeyed through the wilderness,
His wife beside. A mild-faced cow
They drove, and one low-bleating lamb;
He bore a ripe banana-bough,
And she a root of fruitful yam:
This was their worldly worth and store,
But God can make the little more.
The glad earth knew his feet; her mould
Trembled with quickening thrills, and stirred.
Miraculous harvests spread and rolled,
The orchards shone with ruddy gold;
The flocks increased, increased the herd,
And a great nation spread and grew
From the swift lineage of the two,

Peopling the solitary place ;
A fair and strong and fruitful race,
Who knew not pain nor want nor grief,
And Kintu reigned their lord and chief.

So sped three centuries along,
Till Kintu's sons waxed fierce and strong ;
They learned to war, they loved to slay ;
Cruel and dark grew all their faces ;
Discordant death-cries scared the day,
Blood stained the green and holy places ;
And drunk with lust, with anger hot,
His sons mild Kintu heeded not.
At last the god arose in wrath,
His sandals tied, and down the path,
His wife beside him, as of yore,
He went. A cow, a single lamb
They took ; one tuber of the yam ;
One yellow-podded branch they bore
Of ripe banana, — these, no more,
Of all the heaped-up harvest store.
They left the huts, they left the tent,
Nor turned, nor cast a backward look :
Behind, the thick boughs met and shook.

They vanished. Long with wild lament
Mourned all the tribe, in vain, in vain;
The gift once given was given no more,
The grievèd god came not again.

To what far paradise they fared,
That heavenly pair, what wilderness
Their gentle rule next owned and shared,
Knoweth no man, — no man can guess.
On secret roads, by pathways blind,
The gods go forth, and none may find;
But sad the world where God is not!
By man was Kintu soon forgot,
Or named and held as legend dim;
But the wronged earth, remembering him,
By scanty fruit and tardy grain
And silent song revealed her pain.
So centuries came, and centuries went,
And heaped the graves and filled the tent.
Kings rose, and fought their royal way
To conquest over heaps of slain,
And reigned a little. Then, one day,
They vanished into dust again,
And other kings usurped their place,

Who called themselves of Kintu's race,
And worshipped Kintu; not as he,
The mild, benignant deity,
Who held all life a holy thing,
Be it of insect or of king,
Would have ordained, but with wild rite,
With altars heaped, and dolorous cries,
And savage dance, and bale-fires light,
An unaccepted sacrifice.
At last, when thousand years were flown,
The great Ma-anda filled the throne:
A prince of generous heart and high,
Impetuous, noble, fierce, and true;
His wrath like lightning hurtling by,
His pardon like the healing dew.
And chiefs and sages swore each one
He was great Kintu's worthiest son.

One night, in forests still and deep,
A shepherd sat to watch his sheep,
And started, as through darkness dim
A strange voice rang and called to him:
"Wake! there are wonders waiting thee!
Go where the thick mimosas be,

Fringing a little open plain.
Honor and power wouldest thou gain?
Go, foolish man, to fortune blind;
Follow the stream, and thou shalt find."
Three several nights the voice was heard,
Louder and more emphatic grown.
Then, at the thrice-repeated word,
The shepherd rose and went alone,
Threading the mazes of the stream
Like one who wanders in a dream.
Long miles he ran, the stream beside,
Which this way, that way, turned and sped,
And called and sang, a noisy guide.
At last its vagrant dances led
To where the thick mimosas' shade
Circled and fringed an open glade;
There the wild streamlet danced away,
The moon was shining strangely white,
And by its fitful, gleaming ray
The shepherd saw a wondrous sight;
In the glade's midst, each on his mat,
A group of armèd warriors sat,
White-robed, majestic, with deep eyes
Fixed on him with a stern surprise;

And in their midst an aged chief
Enthronèd sat, whose beard, like foam,
Caressed his mighty knees. As leaf
Shakes in the wind the shepherd shook,
And veiled his eyes before that look,
And prayed, and thought upon his home,
Nor spoke, nor moved, till the old man,
In voice like waterfall, began :
" Shepherd, how names himself thy king ? "
" Ma-anda," answered, shuddering,
The shepherd. " Good, thou speakest well.
And now, my son, I bid thee tell
Thy first king's name." " It was Kintu."
" 'T is rightly said, thou answerest true.
Hark ! To Ma-anda, Kintu's son,
Hasten, and bid him, fearing naught,
Come hither, taking thee for guide ;
Thou and he, not another one,
Not even a dog may run beside !
Long has Ma-anda Kintu sought
With spell and conjuration dim,
Now Kintu has a word for him.
Go, do thy errand, haste thee hence,
Kintu insures thy recompense."

All night the shepherd ran, star-led,
All the hot day he hastened straight,
Nor stopped for sleep, nor stopped for bread,
Until he reached the city gate,
And saw red rays of evening fall
On the leaf-hutted capital.
He sought the king, his tale he told.
Ma-anda faltered not, nor stayed.
He seized his spear, he left the tent;
Shook off the brown arms of his queens,
Who clasped his knees with wailing screams;
On pain of instant death forbade
That man should spy or follow him;
And down the pathway, arching dim,
Fearless and light of heart and bold
Followed the shepherd where he went.

But one there was who loved his king
Too well to suffer such strange thing, —
The chieftain of the host was he,
Next to the monarch in degree;
And, fearing wile or stratagem
Menaced the king, he followed them
With noiseless tread and out of sight.

So on they fared the forest through,
From evening shades to dawning light,
From dawning to the dusk and dew, —
The unseen follower and the two.
Ofttimes the king turned back to scan
The path, but never saw he man.
At last the forest-guarded space
They reached, where, ranged in order, sat,
Each couched upon his braided mat,
The white-robed warriors, face to face
With their majestic chief. The king,
Albeit unused to fear or awe,
Bowed down in homage, wondering,
And bent his eyes, as fearing to be
Blinded by rays of deity.
Then asked the mighty voice and calm,
"Art thou Ma-anda called?" "I am."
"And art thou king?" "The king am I,"
The bold Ma-anda made reply.
"'T is rightly spoken; but, my son,
Why hast thou my command forgot,
That no man with thee to this spot
Should come, except thy guide alone?"
"No man has come," Ma-anda said.

"Alone we journeyed, he and I;
And often have I turned my head,
And never living thing could spy.
None is there, on my faith as king."
"A king's word is a weighty thing,"
The old man answered. "Let it be, —
But still a man *has* followed thee!
Now answer, Ma-anda, one more thing:
Who, first of all thy line, was king?"
"Kintu the god." "'T is well, my son,
All creatures Kintu loved, — not one
Too pitiful or weak or small;
He knew them and he loved them all;
And never did a living thing,
Or bird in air or fish in lake,
Endure a pang for Kintu's sake.
Then rose his sons, of differing mind,
Who gorged on cruel feasts each day,
And bathed in blood, and joyed to slay,
And laughed at pain and suffering.
Then Kintu sadly went his way.
The gods long-suffering are and kind,
Often they pardon, long they wait;
But men are evil, men are blind.

After much tarriance, much debate,
The good gods leave them to their fate ;
So Kintu went where none may find.

Each king in turn has sought since then,
From Chora down, the first in line,
To win lost Kintu back to men.
Vain was his search, and vain were thine,
Save that the gods have special grace
To thee, Ma-anda. Face to face
With Kintu thou shalt stand, and he
Shall speak the word of power to thee ;
Clasped to his bosom, thou shalt share
His knowledge of the earth, the air,
And deep things, secret things, shalt learn.
But stay," — the old man's voice grew stern, —
" Before I further speak, declare
Who is that man in ambush there ! "
" There is no man, — no man I see."
" Deny no longer, it is vain.
Within the shadow of the tree
He lurketh ; lo, behold him plain ! "
And the king saw ; — for at the word
From covert stole the hidden spy,

And sought his monarch's side. One cry,
A lion's roar, Ma-anda gave,
Then seized his spear, and poised and drave.
Like lightning bolt it hissed and whirred,
A flash across the midnight blue.
A single groan, a jet of red,
And, pierced and stricken through and through,
Upon the ground the chief fell dead;
But still with love no death could chase,
His eyes sought out his master's face.

Blent with Ma-anda's a wild cry
Of many voices rose on high,
A shriek of anguish and despair,
Which shook and filled the startled air;
And when the king, his wrath still hot,
Turned him, the little grassy plain
All lonely in the moonlight lay:
The chiefs had vanished all away
As melted into thin, blue wind;
Gone was the old man. Stunned and blind,
For a long moment stood the king;
He tried to wake; he rubbed his eyes,
As though some fearful dream to end.

It was no dream, this fearful thing:
There was the forest, there the skies,
The shepherd — and his murdered friend.
With feverish haste, bewildered, mazed,
This way and that he vainly sped,
Beating the air like one half crazed;
With prayers and cries unnumberéd,
Searching, imploring, — vain, all vain.
Only the echoing woods replied,
With mocking booms their long aisles through,
"Come back, Kintu, Kintu, Kintu!"
And pitiless to all his pain
The unanswering gods his suit denied.
At last, as dawning slowly crept
To day, the king sank down and wept
A space; then, lifting as they could
The lifeless burden, once a man,
He and the shepherd-guide began
Their grievous journey through the wood,
The long and hard and dreary way,
Trodden so lightly yesterday;
And the third day, at evening's fall,
Gained the leaf-hutted capital.
There burial rites were duly paid:

Like bridegroom decked for banqueting,
The chief adorned his funeral-pyre ;
Rare gums and spices fed the fire,
Perfumes and every precious thing ;
And songs were sung, and prayers were prayed,
And priests danced jubilant all day.
But prone the king Ma-anda lay,
With ashes on his royal crest,
And groaned, and beat upon his breast,
And called on Kintu loud and wild :
" Father, come back, forgive thy child ! "
Bitter the cry, but vain, all vain ;
The grievéd god came not again.

EASTER.

WHEN dawns on earth the Easter sun
The dear saints feel an answering thrill.
With whitest flowers their hands they fill;
And, singing all in unison,

Unto the battlements they press —
The very marge of heaven — how near!
And bend, and look upon us here
With eyes that rain down tenderness.

Their roses, brimmed with fragrant dew,
Their lilies fair they raise on high;
"Rejoice! The Lord is risen!" they cry;
"Christ is arisen; we prove it true!

"Rejoice, and dry those faithless tears
With which your Easter flowers are stained;
Share in our bliss, who have attained
The rapture of the eternal years;

"Have proved the promise which endures,
The Love that deigned, the Love that died;
Have reached our haven by His side —
Are Christ's, but none the less are yours;

"Yours with a nearness never known
While parted by the veils of sense;
Infinite knowledge, joy intense,
A love which is not love alone,

"But faith perfected, vision free,
And patience limitless and wise —
Beloved, the Lord is risen, arise!
And dare to be as glad as we!"

We do rejoice, we do give thanks,
O blessed ones, for all your gain,
As dimly through these mists of pain
We catch the gleaming of your ranks.

We will arise, with zeal increased,
Blending, the while we strive and grope,
Our paler festival of Hope
With your Fruition's perfect feast.

Bend low, beloved, against the blue ;
  Lift higher still the lilies fair,
  Till, following where our treasures are,
We come to join the feast with you.

BIND-WEED.

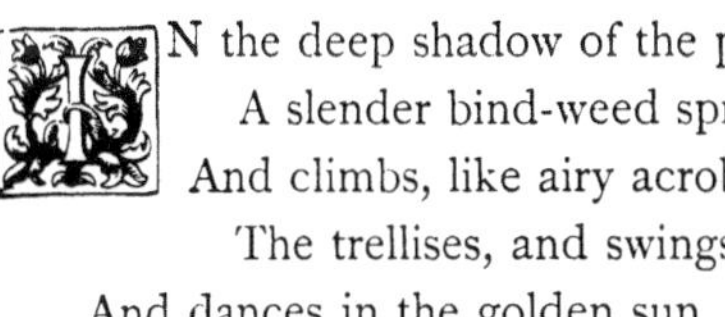

N the deep shadow of the porch
  A slender bind-weed springs,
And climbs, like airy acrobat,
  The trellises, and swings
And dances in the golden sun
  In fairy loops and rings.

Its cup-shaped blossoms, brimmed with dew,
  Like pearly chalices,
Hold cooling fountains, to refresh
  The butterflies and bees;
And humming-birds on vibrant wings
  Hover, to drink at ease.

And up and down the garden-beds,
  Mid box and thyme and yew,
And spikes of purple lavender,
  And spikes of larkspur blue,
The bind-weed tendrils win their way,
  And find a passage through.

With touches coaxing, delicate,
  And arts that never tire,
They tie the rose-trees each to each,
  The lilac to the brier,
Making for graceless things a grace,
  With steady, sweet desire.

Till near and far the garden growths,
  The sweet, the frail, the rude,
Draw close, as if with one consent,
  And find each other good,
Held by the bind-weed's pliant loops,
  In a dear brotherhood.

Like one fair sister, slender, arch,
  A flower in bloom and poise,
Gentle and merry and beloved,
  Making no stir or noise,
But swaying, linking, blessing all
  A family of boys.

APRIL.

HARK ! upon the east-wind, piping, creeping,
Comes a voice all clamorous with despair ;
It is April, crying sore and weeping,
O'er the chilly earth, so brown and bare.

"When I went away," she murmurs, sobbing,
"All my violet-banks were starred with blue ;
Who, O, who has been here, basely robbing
Bloom and odor from the fragrant crew?

"Who has reft the robin's hidden treasure, —
All the speckled spheres he loved so well?
And the buds which danced in merry measure
To the chiming of the hyacinth's bell?

"Where are all my hedge-rows, flushed with Maying?
And the leafy rain, that tossed so fair,
Like the spray from silver fountains playing,
Where the elm-tree's column rose in air?

"All are vanished, and my heart is breaking;
And my tears they slowly drip and fall;
Only death could listen without waking
To the grief and passion of my call!"

Thus she plaineth. Then ten million voices,
Tiny, murmurous, like drops of rain,
Raised in song as when the wind rejoices,
Ring the answer, "We are here again.

"We were hiding, April. Did you miss us?
None of us were really gone away;
Stoop thy pretty head and gently kiss us
Once before we all come out to play.

"Here are all the clustering buds of roses,
And the dandelion's mimic sun;
Of thy much-beloved and vanished posies
None are missing, not a single one!"

Little points of green push out to greet her,
Little creepers grasp her garment's hem,
Hidden sweetnesses grow ever sweeter
As she bends and brightly smiles at them.

Every tear is answered by a blossom,
  Every sigh with songs and laughter blent,
Apple-blooms upon the breezes toss them.
  April knows her own, and is content.

MAY.

NEW flowery scents strewed everywhere,
New sunshine poured in largesse fair,
"We shall be happy now," we say.
A voice just trembles through the air,
And whispers, "May."

Nay, but we *must!* No tiny bud
But thrills with rapture at the flood
Of fresh young life which stirs to-day.
The same wild thrill irradiates our blood;
Why hint of "May"?

For us are coming fast and soon
The delicate witcheries of June;
July, with ankles deep in hay;
The bounteous Autumn. Like a mocking tune
Again sounds, "May."

Spring's last-born darling, clear-eyed, sweet,
Pauses a moment, with white twinkling feet,
  And golden locks in breezy play,
Half teasing and half tender, to repeat
        Her song of "May."

Ah, month of hope ! all promised glee,
All merry meanings, lie in thee ;
  Surely no cloud can daunt thy day.
The ripe lips part in smiling mockery,
        And murmur, "May."

Still from the smile a comfort may we glean ;
Although our "must-be's," "shall-be's," idle seem,
  Close to our hearts one little word we lay :
We may not be as happy as we dream,
        But then we — may.

SECRETS.

N the long, bright summer, dear to bird and bee,
When the woods are standing in liveries green and gay,
Merry little voices sound from every tree,
And they whisper secrets all the day.

If we knew the language, we should hear strange things;
Mrs. Chirry, Mrs. Flurry, deep in private chat.
"How are all your nestlings, dear? Do they use their wings?
What was that sad tale about a cat?"

"Where is your new cottage?" "Hush! I pray you, hush!
Please speak very softly, dear, and make no noise.
It is on the lowest bough of the lilac bush,
And I am so dreadfully afraid of boys.

"Mr. Chirry chose the spot, without consulting me;
Such a very public place, and insecure for it.
I can scarcely sleep at night for nervousness; but he
Says I am a silly thing and does n't mind a bit."

"So the Bluebirds have contracted, have they, for a house?
And a nest is under way for little Mr. Wren?
Hush, dear, hush! Be quiet, dear; quiet as a mouse.
These are weighty secrets, and we must whisper them."

Close the downy dowagers nestle on the bough
While the timorous voices soften low with dread,
And we, walking underneath, little reckon how
Mysteries are couching in the tree-tops overhead.

Ah, the pretty whisperers! It was very well
When the leaves were thick and green, awhile ago —
Leaves are secret-keepers; but since the last leaf fell
There is nothing hidden from the eyes below.

Bared are the brown tenements, and all the world may see
What Mrs. Chirry, Mrs. Flurry, hid so close that day.
In the place of rustling wings, cold winds rustling be,
And thickly lie the icicles where once the warm brood lay.

Shall we tease the birdies, when they come back in spring, —
  Tease and tell them we have fathomed all their secrets small,
Every secret hiding-place and dear and precious thing,
  Which they left behind the leaves, the red leaves, in the fall?

They would only laugh at us and wink their saucy eyes,
  And answer, "Last year's secrets are all past and told.
New years bring new happenings and fresh mysteries,
  You are very welcome to the stale ones of the old!"

HOW THE LEAVES CAME DOWN.

I'LL tell you how the leaves came down.
The great Tree to his children said,
"You 're getting sleepy, Yellow and Brown,
Yes, very sleepy, little Red;
It is quite time you went to bed."

"Ah!" begged each silly, pouting leaf,
"Let us a little longer stay;
Dear Father Tree, behold our grief,
'T is such a very pleasant day
We do not want to go away."

So, just for one more merry day
To the great Tree the leaflets clung,
Frolicked and danced and had their way,
Upon the autumn breezes swung,
Whispering all their sports among,

"Perhaps the great Tree will forget
  And let us stay until the spring,
If we all beg and coax and fret."
  But the great Tree did no such thing;
  He smiled to hear their whispering.

"Come, children all, to bed," he cried;
  And ere the leaves could urge their prayer
He shook his head, and far and wide,
  Fluttering and rustling everywhere,
  Down sped the leaflets through the air.

I saw them; on the ground they lay,
  Golden and red, a huddled swarm,
Waiting till one from far away,
  White bed-clothes heaped upon her arm,
  Should come to wrap them safe and warm.

The great bare Tree looked down and smiled.
  "Good-night, dear little leaves," he said;
And from below each sleepy child
  Replied "Good-night," and murmured,
  "It is *so* nice to go to bed."

BARCAROLES.

I.

OVER the lapsing lagune all the day
  Urging my gondola with oar-strokes light,
Always beside one shadowy waterway
  I pause and peer, with eager, jealous sight,
Toward the Piazza where Pepita stands,
  Wooing the hungry pigeons from their flight.

Dark the canal; but she shines like the sun,
  With yellow hair and dreaming, wine-brown eyes.
Thick crowd the doves for food. She gives *me* none.
  She sees and will not see. Vain are my sighs.
One slow, reluctant stroke. Aha! she turns,
  Gestures and smiles, with coy and feigned surprise.

Shifting and baffling is our Lido track,
  Blind and bewildering all the currents flow.
Me they perplex not. In the midnight black
  I hold my way secure and fearless row.
But ah! what chart have I to her, my Sea,
  Whose fair, mysterious depths I long to know?

Subtle as sad mirage; true and untrue
  She seems, and, pressing ever on in vain,
I yearn across the mocking, tempting blue.
  Never she draws more near, never I gain
A furlong's space toward where she sits and smiles;
  Smiles and cares nothing for my love and pain.

How shall I win her? What may strong arm do
  Against such gentle distance? I can say
No more than this, that when she stands to woo
  The doves beside the shadowy waterway,
And when I look and long, sometimes — she smiles!
  Perhaps she will do more than smile one day!

II.

LIGHT and darkness, brown and fair,
  Ha ! they think I do not see, —
I behind them, swiftly rowing.
  Rowing? Yes, but eyes are free,
    Eyes and fancies : —

Now what fire in looks and glances !
  Now the dark head bends, grown bolder.
Ringlets mingle — silence — broken
  (All unconscious of beholder)
    By a kiss !

What could lovers ask or miss
  In such moonlight, such June weather,
But a boat like this, (me rowing !)
  And forever and together
    To be floating?

Ah ! if she and I such boating
  Might but share one day, some fellow
With strong arms behind, Pasquale,
  Or Luigi, with gay awning,
    (She likes yellow !)

She — I mean Pepita — mellow
  Moonlight on the waves, no other
To break silence or catch whispers,
  All the love which now I smother
    Told and spoken, —

Listened to, a kiss for token :
  How, my Signor? What! so soon
Homeward bound? We, born of Venice,
  Live by night and nap by noon.
    If 't were me, now,

With *my* brown-eyed girl, this prow
  Would not turn for hours still ;
But the Signor bids, *commandi!*
  I am here to do his will,
    He is master.

Glide we on ; so, faster, faster.
  Now the two are safely landed.
Buono mano, grazie, Signor,
  They who love are open-handed.
    Now, Pepita!

III.

TORCELLO.

SHE has said " yes," and the world is a-smile.
There she sits as she sat in my dream ;
There she sits, and the blue waves gleam,
And the current bears us along the while
For happy mile after happy mile,
A fairy boat on a fairy stream.

The Angelus bells swing to and fro,
And the sunset lingers to hear their swell,
For the sunset loves such music well.
A big, bright moon is hovering low,
Where the edge of the sky is all aglow,
Like the middle heart of a red, red shell.

The Lido floats like a purple flower ;
Orange and rose are the sails at sea ;
Silver and pink the surf-line free

Tumbles and chimes, and the perfect hour
Clasps us and folds us in its power,
   Folds us and holds us, my love and me.

Can there be sadness anywhere
   In the world to-night? Or tears or sighs
   Beneath such festal moon and skies?
Can there be memory or despair?
What is it, beloved? Why point you there,
   With sudden dew in those dearest eyes?

Yes! one sad thing on the happy earth!
   Like a mourner's veil in the bridal array,
   Or a sorrowful sigh in the music gay,
A shade on the sun, in the feast a dearth,
   Drawn like a ghost across our way,
Torcello sits and rebukes our mirth.

She sits a widow who sat as queen,
   Ashes on brows once crowned and bright;
   Woe in the eyes once full of light;
Her sad, fair roses and manifold green,
   All bitter and pallid and heavy with night,
Are full of the shadows of woes unseen.

Let us hurry away from her face unblest,
  Row us away, for the song is done,
  The Angelus bells cease, one by one,
Pepita's head lies on my breast;
But, trembling and full of a vague unrest,
  I long for the morrow and for the sun.

MY RIGHTS.

YES, God has made me a woman,
And I am content to be
Just what He meant, not reaching out
For other things, since He
Who knows me best and loves me most has ordered this for me.

A woman, to live my life out
In quiet womanly ways,
Hearing the far-off battle,
Seeing as through a haze
The crowding, struggling world of men fight through their busy days.

I am not strong or valiant,
I would not join the fight
Or jostle with crowds in the highways
To sully my garments white ;
But I have rights as a woman, and here I claim my right.

The right of a rose to bloom
In its own sweet, separate way,
With none to question the perfumed pink
And none to utter a nay
If it reaches a root or points a thorn, as even a rose-tree may.

The right of the lady-birch to grow,
To grow as the Lord shall please,
By never a sturdy oak rebuked,
Denied nor sun nor breeze,
For all its pliant slenderness, kin to the stronger trees.

The right to a life of my own, —
Not merely a casual bit
Of somebody else's life, flung out
That, taking hold of it,
I may stand as a cipher does after a numeral writ.

The right to gather and glean
What food I need and can
From the garnered store of knowledge
Which man has heaped for man,
Taking with free hands freely and after an ordered plan.

The right — ah, best and sweetest ! —
To stand all undismayed
Whenever sorrow or want or sin
Call for a woman's aid,
With none to cavil or question, by never a look gainsaid.

I do not ask for a ballot ;
Though very life were at stake,
I would beg for the nobler justice
That men for manhood's sake
Should give ungrudgingly, nor withhold till I must fight and take.

The fleet foot and the feeble foot
Both seek the self-same goal,
The weakest soldier's name is writ
On the great army-roll,
And God, who made man's body strong, made too the woman's soul.

SOLSTICE.

I.

SIT at evening's scented close,
In fulness of the summer-tide ;
All dewy fair the lily glows,
No single petal of the rose
Has fallen to dim the rose's pride.

Sweet airs, sweet harmonies of hue,
Surround, caress me everywhere ;
The spells of dusk, the spells of dew,
My senses steal, my reason woo,
And sing a lullaby to care.

But vainly do the warm airs sing,
All vain the roses' rapturous breath ;
A chill blast, as from wintry wing,
Smites on my heart, and, shuddering,
I see the beauty changed to death.

Afar I see it loom and rise,
That pitiless and icy shape.
It blots the blue, it dims the skies;
Amid the summer land it cries,
"I come, and there is no escape!"

O, bitter drop in bloom and sweet!
O, canker on the smiling day!
Have we but climbed the hill to meet
Thy fronting face, thy eyes of sleet?
To hate, yet dare not turn away?

II.

I sit beneath a leaden sky,
Amid the piled and drifted snow;
My feet are on the graves where lie
The roses which made haste to die
So long, so very long ago.

The sobbing wind is fierce and strong,
Its cry is like a human wail,
But in my heart it sings this song:
"Not long, O Lord! O Lord, not long!
Surely thy spring-time shall prevail."

Out of the darkness and the cold,
  Out of the wintry depths I lean,
And lovingly I clasp and hold
The promises, and see unrolled
  A vision of the summer green.

O, life in death, sweet plucked from pain !
  O, distant vision fair to see !
Up the long hill we press and strain ;
We can bear all things and attain,
  If once our faces turn to Thee !

IN THE MIST.

SITTING all day in a silver mist,
   In silver silence all the day,
   Save for the low, soft hiss of spray,
And the lisp of sands by waters kissed,
   As the tide draws up the bay.

Little I hear and nothing I see,
   Wrapped in that veil by fairies spun;
The solid earth is vanished for me,
And the shining hours speed noiselessly,
   A web of shadow and sun.

Suddenly out of the shifting veil
   A magical bark, by the sunbeams lit,
   Flits like a dream, — or seems to flit, —
With a golden prow and a gossamer sail,
   And the waves make room for it.

A fair, swift bark from some radiant realm,
  Its diamond cordage cuts the sky
  In glittering lines; all silently
A seeming spirit holds the helm
  And steers: will he pass me by?

Ah, not for me is the vessel here!
  Noiseless and fast as a sea-bird's flight,
  She swerves and vanishes from my sight;
No flap of sail, no parting cheer, —
  She has passed into the light.

Sitting some day in a deeper mist,
  Silent, alone, some other day,
  An unknown bark from an unknown bay,
By unknown waters lapped and kissed,
  Shall near me through the spray.

No flap of sail, no scraping of keel:
  Shadowy, dim, with a banner dark,
It will hover, will pause, and I shall feel
A hand which beckons, and, shivering, steal
  To the cold strand and embark.

Embark for that far mysterious realm,
  Whence the fathomless, trackless waters flow.
  Shall I see a Presence dim, and know
A Gracious Hand upon the helm,
  Nor be afraid to go?

And through black wave and stormy blast,
  And out of the fog-wreath dense and dun,
  Guided and held, shall the vessel run,
Gain the fair haven, night being past,
  And anchor in the sun?

WITHIN.

COULD my heart hold another one?
I cannot tell.
Sometimes it seems an ample dome,
Sometimes a cell.

Sometimes a temple filled with saints,
Serene and fair,
Whose eyes are pure from mortal taints
As lilies are.

Sometimes a narrow shrine, in which
One precious face
Smiles ever from its guarded niche,
With deathless grace.

Sometimes a nest, where weary things,
And weak and shy,
Are brooded under mother wings
Till they can fly.

And then a palace, with wide rooms
Adorned and dressed,
Where eager slaves pour sweet perfumes
For each new guest.

Whiche'er it be, I know always
Within that door —
Whose latch it is not mine to raise —
Blows evermore,

With breath of balm upon its wing,
A soft, still air,
Which makes each closely folded thing
Look always fair.

My darlings, do you feel me near,
As every day
Into this hidden place and dear
I take my way?

Always you stand in radiant guise,
Always I see
A noiseless welcome in the eyes
You turn on me.

And, whether I come soon or late,
        Whate'er befall,
Always within the guarded gate
        I find you all.

MENACE.

ALL green and fair the Summer lies,
Just budded from the bud of Spring,
With tender blue of wistful skies,
And winds which softly sing.

Her clock has struck its morning hours;
Noon nears — the flowery dial is true;
But still the hot sun veils its powers,
In deference to the dew.

Yet there amid the fresh new green,
Amid the young broods overhead,
A single scarlet branch is seen,
Swung like a banner red;

Tinged with the fatal hectic flush
Which, when October frosts are near,
Flames on each dying tree and bush,
To deck the dying year.

And now the sky seems not so blue,
  The yellow sunshine pales its ray,
A sorrowful, prophetic hue
  Lies on the radiant day,

As mid the bloom and tenderness
  I catch that scarlet menace there,
Like a gray sudden wintry tress
  Set in a child's bright hair.

The birds sing on, the roses blow,
  But like a discord heard but now.
A stain upon the petal's snow
  Is that one sad, red bough.

"HE THAT BELIEVETH SHALL NOT MAKE HASTE."

THE aloes grow upon the sand,
The aloes thirst with parching heat;
Year after year they waiting stand,
Lonely and calm, and front the beat
Of desert winds; and still a sweet
And subtle voice thrills all their veins:
"Great patience wins; it still remains,
After a century of pains,
To you to bloom and be complete."

I grow upon a thorny waste;
Hot noontide lies on all the way,
And with its scorching breath makes haste
Each freshening dawn to burn and slay,
Yet patiently I bide and stay:
Knowing the secret of my fate,
The hour of bloom, dear Lord, I wait,
Come when it will, or soon or late,
A hundred years are but a day.

MY LITTLE GHOST.

 KNOW where it lurks and hides,
In the midst of the busy house,
In the midst of the children's glee,
All day its shadow bides:
Nobody knows but me.

On a closet-shelf it dwells,
In the darkest corner of all,
Mid rolls of woollen and fur,
And faint, forgotten smells
Of last year's lavender.

That a ghost has its dwelling there
Nobody else would guess, —
"Only a baby's shoe,
A curl of golden hair,"
You would say, "a toy or two, —

"A broken doll, whose lips
  And cheeks of waxen bloom
  Show dents of fingers small, —
Little, fair finger-tips, —
  A worn sash, — that is all."

Little to see or to guess;
  But whenever I open the door,
  There, faithful to its post,
With its eyes' sad tenderness,
  I see my little ghost.

And I hasten to shut the door,
  I shut it tight and fast,
  Lest the sweet, sad thing get free,
Lest it flit beside on the floor,
  And sadden the day for me,

Lest between me and the sun,
  And between me and the heavens,
  And the laugh in the children's eyes,
The shadowy feet should run,
  The faint gold curls arise

Like a gleam of moonlight pale,
  And all the warmth and the light
  Should die from the summer day,
And the laughter turn to wail,
  And I should forget to pray.

So I keep the door shut fast,
  And my little ghost shut in,
  And whenever I cross the hall
I shiver and hurry past;
  But I love it best of all.

CHRISTMAS.

HOW did they keep his birthday then,
 The little fair Christ, so long ago?
 O, many there were to be housed and fed,
And there was no place in the inn, they said,
 So into the manger the Christ must go,
To lodge with the cattle and not with men.

The ox and the ass they munched their hay,
 They munched and they slumbered, wondering not,
And out in the midnight cold and blue
The shepherds slept, and the sheep slept too,
 Till the angels' song and the bright star ray
Guided the wise men to the spot.

But only the wise men knelt and praised,
 And only the shepherds came to see,
And the rest of the world cared not at all
For the little Christ in the oxen's stall;
 And we are angry and amazed
That such a dull, hard thing should be!

How do we keep his birthday now?
  We ring the bells and we raise the strain,
We hang up garlands everywhere
And bid the tapers twinkle fair,
  And feast and frolic — and then we go
Back to the same old lives again.

Are we so better, then, than they
  Who failed the new-born Christ to see?
To them a helpless babe, — to us
He shines a Saviour glorious,
  Our Lord, our Friend, our All — yet we
Are half asleep this Christmas day.

BENEDICAM DOMINO.

THANK God for life : life is not sweet always.
Hands may be heavy-laden, hearts care full,
Unwelcome nights follow unwelcome days,
And dreams divine end in awakenings dull.
Still it is life, and life is cause for praise.
This ache, this restlessness, this quickening sting,
Prove me no torpid and inanimate thing,
Prove me of Him who is of life the Spring.
I am alive ! — and that is beautiful.

Thank God for Love : though Love may hurt and wound
Though set with sharpest thorns its rose may be,
Roses are not of winter, all attuned
Must be the earth, full of soft stir, and free
And warm ere dawns the rose upon its tree.
Fresh currents through my frozen pulses run ;
My heart has tasted summer, tasted sun,
And I can thank Thee, Lord, although not one
Of all the many roses blooms for me.

Thank God for Death : bright thing with dreary name,
We wrong with mournful flowers her pure, still brow.
We heap her with reproaches and with blame,
Her goodness and her fitness disallowed,
Questioning bitterly her why and how.
But calmly mid her clamor and surmise
She touches each in turn, and each grows wise.
Taught by the light in her mysterious eyes,
I *shall* be glad, and I am thankful now.

MAY 6 1919

University Press: John Wilson & Son, Cambridge.

www.ingramcontent.com/pod-product-compliance
Lightning Source LLC
LaVergne TN
LVHW011229110826
845150LV00006B/1588

9781425514938